WINERY DOGS

OF NAPA VALLEY

Photography by **Andrea Jacoby & Heather Zundel**

Text by **Elaine Riordan**

Published by Winery Dogs Publishing
Hardcover, Second Edition
First printing July 2006

ISBN: 0-9773041-0-8

Address correspondence or orders to:
Winery Dogs Publishing
sales@winerydogs.com

Individual books may be purchased at:
www.winerydogs.com

Photography by Andrea Jacoby and Heather Zundel
Foreword by Andrea Jacoby
Text by Elaine Riordan

Design by Createffects Inc.
(404) 921-3338

Printed in Korea by Asianprinting.com

Winery Dogs of Napa Valley is a proud supporter of PAWS (Pets are Wonderful Support).

PAWS is a volunteer-based organization that provides for the comprehensive needs of companion animals for low-income persons with HIV/AIDS and other disabling illnesses. By providing these essential support services, educating the larger community on the benefits of the human-animal bond, and advocating for the rights of disabled individuals to keep service animals, PAWS improves the health and well-being of disabled individuals and the animals in their lives.

Dogs remind us of what we value most: the joy of unguarded affection and the peace of quiet companionship. We dedicate this book to our dogs, past and present, who have given us so much happiness—Wesley, Mulligan, McGee, Jock, Gidget, Ambro, Corky, Casey, Josie and Pops.

Winery Dogs of Napa Valley

Table of Contents

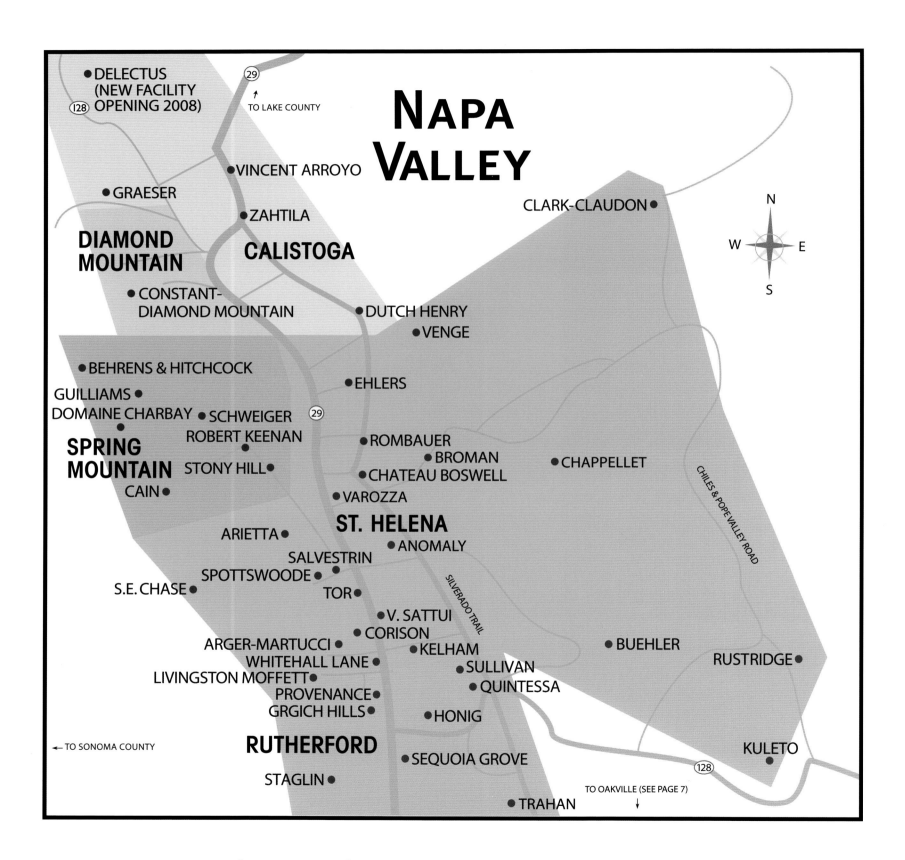

NAPA VALLEY

● DELECTUS
(NEW FACILITY
OPENING 2008)

29
↑
TO LAKE COUNTY

●VINCENT ARROYO

●GRAESER

●ZAHTILA

CLARK-CLAUDON ●

**DIAMOND
MOUNTAIN**

CALISTOGA

N
W ✦ E
S

●CONSTANT-
DIAMOND MOUNTAIN

●DUTCH HENRY
●VENGE

●BEHRENS & HITCHCOCK

●EHLERS

GUILLIAMS ●
DOMAINE CHARBAY ●SCHWEIGER
●
**SPRING
MOUNTAIN** ●ROBERT KEENAN
STONY HILL●
CAIN ●

29

●ROMBAUER
●BROMAN
●CHATEAU BOSWELL
●VAROZZA

●CHAPPELLET

CHILES & POPE VALLEY ROAD

ST. HELENA
●ANOMALY

ARIETTA ●

SALVESTRIN
SPOTTSWOODE ●
S.E. CHASE ● TOR ●

SILVERADO TRAIL

●V. SATTUI
●CORISON
ARGER-MARTUCCI ●
WHITEHALL LANE ●
LIVINGSTON MOFFETT●
PROVENANCE●
GRGICH HILLS●

●KELHAM
●SULLIVAN
●QUINTESSA

●BUEHLER

RUSTRIDGE ●

●HONIG

← TO SONOMA COUNTY

RUTHERFORD

STAGLIN ●

●SEQUOIA GROVE

KULETO
●

128

TO OAKVILLE (SEE PAGE 7)
↓

●TRAHAN

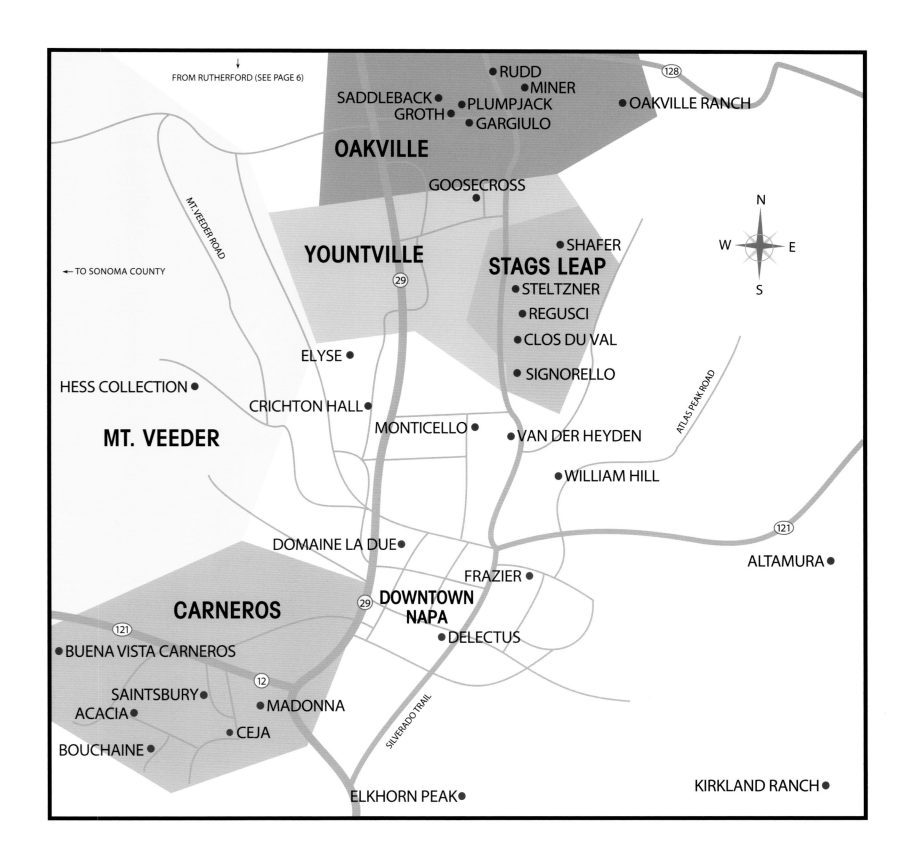

Winery Dogs of Napa Valley

FOREWORD

People always say, "Do what you love to do." So my husband, Allen, and I merged two of our passions—wine and dogs—and set out to publish a book about the two. It was also a perfect way for me to indulge a third passion of mine, photography, and a wonderful excuse to revisit the breathtaking wine country of Napa Valley. With help from our talented family—my sister Heather (co-photographer and marketing manager) and cousin Elaine (writer, editor, and source of never-ending information about the world of publishing)—this book was born.

At first we envisioned the book's subject matter would be fifty percent about the dogs and fifty percent about the wineries. What we quickly learned during our visits and interviews, however, was that it's impossible to separate the two. Winery dogs are inextricably connected to the culture, spirit, and essence of the wineries they call home. We never expected to meet so many interesting people and hear so many inspirational stories about the wineries and the families that own them. We wish we could have said more about these amazing wineries and families in our book, but we were limited by space. Therefore, we have devoted our pages to the beauty and exuberance of every winery dog we met. Perhaps our next book should be titled *Winery Families of Napa Valley.*

Unlike most other dogs, winery dogs go to work with people, day by day, at the wineries and in the vineyards, inside and outside, making guests happy and traipsing through the vines. With so much interaction between dogs and family members, employees, and guests, the connection these dogs have to the wineries takes on a special significance. As Jon Frazier of Frazier Winery told us, the right dog brings something spiritual to the whole operation. And at seventy-four wineries in Napa Valley, we saw this was true. Dogs bring out the best in people, and then people give their best selves to the wine. How can the winemaking process not be positively influenced by these loving dogs?

From tiny toy poodles to rottweilers and bull mastiffs, winery dogs come in all shapes and sizes. They arrive at wineries as puppies or adults. They come from breeders, friends, shelters, or newspaper ads. They are surprises on doorsteps, in garbage cans, or under bridges. They are shy or bold, mellow or full of energy. And in no time, whatever their size and origin and temperament, they fit right in.

Winery dogs are greeters, tasters, entertainers, herders, healers, protectors, hunters, chasers, celebrities, and sales enhancers. Older dogs train the new ones, bigger dogs protect the smaller ones, and all of them get on remarkably well with the winery cats. They ride in winery vehicles; they run beside employees in the fields; they sit nicely as visitors arrive for tastings. Better companions would be hard to find.

To see and experience the gifts these dogs bring to the wineries was instantly rewarding for us, and every memory just compounds the good feeling. We would like to thank everyone we met at the wineries for the warm receptions, lively conversations, patience, encouragement, and delicious wine. The welcoming people of Napa Valley have made our project a journey we will always treasure. We hope that everyone who reads *Winery Dogs of Napa Valley* will experience the same affection and inspiration we felt at every winery we were privileged to visit.

Calistoga

Delectus Winery

Dutch Henry Winery

Graeser Estate & Winery

Vincent Arroyo Winery

Zahtila Vineyards

Diamond Mountain

CONSTANT–Diamond Mountain Vineyard & Winery

Flash

FLASH & FANNIE MAE
DELECTUS WINERY

Flash and Fannie Mae always impress guests with their running speed in the vineyards, but few know about their interactions with Gerhard, Linda, and Julia Reisacher's other animals on the property. When Bob the water turtle's tank is being cleaned, Flash—an eleven-year-old Australian shepherd—steps in to be sure the turtle won't wander into trouble. One time Flash sniffed Bob's head too closely, and Bob bit Flash's tongue, holding on tight. Flash howled in pain, shaking his head left and right, but Bob refused to let go. Finally, Flash batted Bob off with a steady paw and learned instantly to respect Bob's space. Fannie Mae—a two-year-old Border collie—loves the neighboring burros and keeps them company, playing with them every chance she gets. Two Delectus wines, the 2002 Dog-Gone Good and the 2003 Dog In Style, feature Flash on the label. Future vintages will include Fannie Mae and other well-loved pets.

Sadie

14

Buggsy

Sissy

Henry

BUGGSY, SADIE, HENRY & SISSY
DUTCH HENRY WINERY

Weekday visitors to the Dutch Henry Winery are greeted by winemaker Scott Chafen's two vivacious Airedale terriers: Lady Buggsy of Blue Acre-Avalon, with distinctive white paws, and Avalon's Lady Pink Sadie, whose curvy tail can be seen wagging from a distance. Visitors who don't watch their bags may be surprised to see Sadie running off with their water bottles—Sadie loves toys, but she loves visitors' water bottles more. Weekend visitors are greeted not only by Buggsy and Sadie, but by winery owner Less Chafen's pugs, Henry and Sissy. During the week, Henry and Sissy work with Maggie Chafen at Dottie Dolittle, a children's clothing store in San Francisco, greeting customers and making children laugh. At Dutch Henry, away from the busy world of retail sales, they have more room to run around, but they still race to greet winery visitors, never tiring of being petted.

OUTSIDE THE BOUNDARIES SERIES
2002
ALEX'S RUFF RED
TABLE WINE
NORTH COAST

ALEX
GRAESER ESTATE AND WINERY

Managing the Graeser estate is something that Alex, a ten-year-old German shepherd, never gets tired of. Early each morning, he accompanies owner and winemaker Richard Graeser on a "vineyard management walk" along the steep hillside vineyards, checking the progress of the vines and taking in the morning air. After chasing away birds and deer, Alex checks the irrigation sprinklers that feed the surrounding gardens—having fun in the water whenever the mood strikes. A conscientious manager at the winery, Alex greets guests between naps at the front door and works up an appetite running after the delivery men. Alex even helps inspire the winemaking. Alex's Ruff Red, a tasty red table wine, is the newest in Graeser's series of dog-inspired wines.

Winery Dogs of Napa Valley

Bodega

J.J.

J.J. & BODEGA
VINCENT ARROYO WINERY

A customer gave J.J., now a six-year-old black Labrador retriever, to winery owner and winemaker Vincent Arroyo. Like Joy, the Greenwood Ranch's previous black Labrador retriever, J.J. is an inspiration, an entertainer, and a wine connoisseur. In her best role, she inspires Vincent to create the red table wine he calls J.J.'s Blend. "You can't make wine without a dog," says Vincent. She is also a masterful entertainer, climbing on wine barrels to catch tennis balls that guests throw to her. After watching people taste wine all day, she unwinds with a glass of red wine poured over her lamb-and-rice dinner each evening. Bodega, a five-month-old chocolate Labrador retriever, enjoys long visits to the winery when Adrian and Matt Moye, Vincent's daughter and son-in-law, come to work. Unfortunately for Vincent, Bodega chews whatever she finds, including his office files. New file cabinets with locks are on order.

ZOE
ZAHTILA VINEYARDS

Zoe, Laura Zahtila's gentle five-year-old yellow Labrador retriever, is a natural at greeting visitors. It's no surprise that Zoe's mother, a yellow Labrador at RustRidge Ranch and Winery, is a renowned greeter as well. Zoe belonged at Zahtila right away—she laid her head on Laura's shoulder the moment they met, and Laura's nephews quickly named her. Today, Zoe not only greets the workers in the vineyard and tasting room, but she welcomes guests as their cars arrive at the winery. Lying on the front deck, sometimes in the sun and sometimes in the shade, she waits for the sound of tires on the gravel. Before the car is even parked, Zoe is waiting by the driver's door with a squeaky toy in her mouth, wagging her tail and hoping to be petted. She leads visitors to the tasting room and stays with them until they feel at home. Then she assumes her position on the deck, listening for the sound of the next approaching engine.

Caso

CASO & FLOOZY
CONSTANT–Diamond Mountain Vineyard & Winery

At CONSTANT–Diamond Mountain Winery, the two Portuguese water dogs take their jobs at the winery seriously. Caso de Vino, twelve years old and recently blind, is director of tasting. When he begins eating the Cabernet Sauvignon grapes in the vineyard, winery owners Fred and Mary Constant know their grapes are ripe. Caso (which in Portuguese means "lover") was "awesome in his day," says Fred—no deer was safe in the vineyards when Caso was there. Caso's companion, the equally beautiful two-year-old Floozy Fairbanks, is the director of hospitality. At the sorting table, she monitors the sorting of grapes to be sure they're perfect, and with guests, she takes the lead to make sure they feel comfortable. When Fred takes visitors in his Swiss Army troop carrier on a 45-minute thrill ride through one of Napa's highest vineyards, Floozy—who is shameless about her love of affection, even in a bumpy vehicle—keeps the visitors from getting too nervous. Floozy and Caso both demonstrate their love of the land, as well as the stunning swimming pools, and visitors who watch them gracefully run and swim can't help but enjoy themselves, too.

Carneros

Acacia Vineyard
Bouchaine Vineyards
Buena Vista Carneros Winery
Ceja Vineyards
Madonna Estate Winery
Saintsbury

Mt. Veeder

Hess Collection Vineyards

Riley

Roxy

Jellybean

JELLYBEAN, RILEY & ROXY
ACACIA VINEYARD

Jellybean, Riley, and Roxy are comical characters—each one an oddball. Jellybean, a seven-year-old mutt, loves to greet people "wearing her white shoes," says winery chef Kevin Simonson, referring to Jellybean's black legs and white paws. However, if someone has a ball in hand, she is powerless to do anything but stare at it, for hours, if need be, until it's in play. Riley, a four-year-old black Labrador retriever mix, is nicknamed "Jerry Rice" because of his ability to hone in on the ball and always make the catch, says Mike Beguelin, Acacia's official Man of Luxury and Leisure. Riley does his best to agitate Roxy, an eleven-year-old yellow Labrador retriever mix, but Roxy—a mellow presence and an agile swimmer—does her best to resist. Roxy has a keen sense of smell and spends hours sniffing the ground. In honor of their funny dogs, Acacia produces a limited quantity of a red table wine known as Mongrel Rouge.

MONGREL ROUGE

CALIFORNIA TABLE WINE
Undistinguished Pedigree & Uncertain Lineage

13% ALC BY VOLUME CONTAINS SULFITES
PRODUCED AND BOTTLED BY ACACIA WINERY, NAPA, CA

EARL
BOUCHAINE VINEYARDS

Earl, a mutt—possibly part rottweiler and part German shepherd—lives in the moment. Abandoned as a puppy on July 4 at Acacia Vineyard, he was quickly adopted by Bill Murray, a former Acacia employee who is now Bouchaine's associate winemaker. Earl walks to work on his own schedule and leaves by his own time clock. One day when an Oakland news reporter arrived at the vineyards, Earl suddenly leapt on the reporter's three-wheeler and accompanied him during the live filming. These days Earl darts out to join Bill, an avid marathoner, for a mile or two of running, exhibiting obvious pleasure in every step.

TRIXIE
BUENA VISTA CARNEROS WINERY

Trixie, a one-year-old Border collie, has one mission: to keep Charlie O'Brien in line. She loves to run through the vineyards, chase the rabbits, and torment the chickens and gophers, but she always races back to check on Charlie, the maintenance technician for all equipment inside the winery. She's extremely protective of him and his children. Even when there is no one staying at the winery's guest house, she circles through the yard to maintain her sphere of influence. Once, when Charlie left for a few days, she stayed with Charlie's friend Mike. Desperate to see what Charlie was up to, though, she dug a tunnel under Mike's property and ran at breakneck speed to find him. Charlie wonders if he'll ever get to go away again.

Winery Dogs of Napa Valley

BRUJA
CEJA VINEYARDS

Bruja, a nine-year-old Alaskan husky/Australian shepherd mix, is an essential part of the winery's hospitality team. Though *bruja* means "witch" in Spanish, it also carries the connotation of *curandera*, which means "healer." As vineyard owner Amelia Ceja says, "she really makes everyone around her feel better." Bruja warmly welcomes guests, understands both English and Spanish, and accompanies winemaker Armando Ceja on vineyard tours. When she's not with guests, Bruja chases rabbits from the vineyard, monitors the coming and going of other dogs, savors Pinot Noir grapes, and enjoys gourmet food. After a long day at work, she appreciates her favorite meal of grilled boneless and skinless chicken breasts marinated in olive oil, lime juice, garlic, and Spanish saffron.

Jethro (front),
Ellie May & Shasta

34

Dodger

JETHRO, ELLIE MAY, SHASTA, ZOE & DODGER
MADONNA ESTATE WINERY

Most of the six dogs at the Madonna Estate Winery have tragic histories. Jethro and Ellie May, both ten-year-old redbone hound mixes, were found abandoned as puppies in the Bartolucci family's garbage cans. Shasta, an eight-year-old greyhound/afghan/wolf mix, was an inheritance from Andrea Bartolucci's parents. Jake (not pictured), a six-year-old redbone hound/collie mix, was adopted via a newspaper advertisement. Zoe, a five-year-old mutt, was found abandoned at a pet store, and Dodger, a two-year-old mutt and "natural star," came from a shelter in Hollywood. The Bartolucci family lightheartedly suggests that their once-sad dogs represent the souls of lost people, comparing them to the stray dogs that wander the ruins of Pompeii, Italy. Today the family has built a new home modeled after an Italian villa, and one beautiful painted mural features happy wandering dogs.

Zoe

Champ

CHAMP & SCOUT
SAINTSBURY

Champ and Scout, both seven-year-old Border collies, were adopted from a cardboard box outside a Target in Vallejo. At the vineyards, both like to chase rabbits and balls for hours. At a winery-owned ranch on Henry Road, they herd the cattle, which involves a lot of barking, chasing, and rolling in cow patties. Sometimes they get so carried away that they herd the winery cats, Beau and Ralph, as well. "Champ and Scout keep us grounded and amused," say general manager David Graves and his wife, Elizabeth McKinney. "They're a constant source of comfort and companionship."

ROWDY
HESS COLLECTION VINEYARDS

If there were no vehicles at the vineyards, Rowdy—a nine-month-old Catahoula hound from Ukiah—would run free all day, taking quick breaks to rest on the quiet, shady hills with the loveliest views. But once an ATV revs up, Rowdy runs as if he's at the races, chasing the tires as far as they go. Inside a truck, Rowdy desperately wants to drive; once he even took the wheel from Bob, a tractor mechanic, and now Bob knows to grip the wheel tightly and keep one eye on Rowdy. Bob hopes that one day Rowdy will find other interests. With luck, Rowdy will soon chase deer from the vineyards, settle down enough to be petted and admired, and leave the ATVs alone once in a while.

Napa County

Altamura Winery and Vineyards

Crichton Hall Vineyard

Domaine La Due

Elkhorn Peak Cellars

Elyse Winery

Frazier Winery

Kirkland Ranch Winery

Monticello Vineyards

Van Der Heyden Vineyards

William Hill Winery

WOODY
ALTAMURA WINERY AND VINEYARDS

Woody, a seven-year-old Hovawart, is calm around visitors, lying at their feet and always ready to be petted. For the most part, he's very laid-back, choosing to drink red wine (for his heart), riding in the Jeep with winery owners Frank and Karen Altamura, or sleeping on the cave's cool floor. But big birds set him off. Woody spends hours chasing turkeys from the vineyards, and he tries in vain to catch egrets sitting placidly on the treetops. Sometimes buzzards circle above the property in large loops. Below them Woody circles, too, making sure they don't touch down.

PUMPKIN
CRICHTON HALL VINEYARD

Pumpkin, a fourteen-year-old chow/golden retriever mix, has led an adventurous life with general manager Tina Bump. Adopted from an Atlanta shelter when she was seven months old, Pumpkin lived in Oklahoma and Colorado when Tina was marketing director of USA Wrestling. For a time, Pumpkin got quite a workout when she stayed with a heavyweight wrestler and a basketball player. Happy today in Napa Valley, Pumpkin spends most days watching the turkeys in the barn or waiting for visitors on the shady deck. A protector of the vines, she chases squirrels and wild turkeys from the property and enjoys her reward of hand-fed grapes.

CHIANTI
DOMAINE LA DUE

Chianti, a four-year-old golden retriever, is a joyful best friend to winery owners Douglas and Angela Due. In the vineyards, Chianti loves to run free and to watch Angela's father, John Guman, on the tractor as it ambles past the vines at the base of Mt. George. At home alone on her favorite leather chair, she keeps watch over the neighborhood, but she's not a guard dog. "If a burglar came to the house," Angela jokes, "she would probably help him carry out the VCR." When Doug and Angela come home, Chianti—ready to burst with excitement—dances as they walk in the door. And when Doug sings, Chianti sings along, her beautiful brown eyes full of love for her family.

Cody

MAGGIE & CODY
ELKHORN PEAK CELLARS

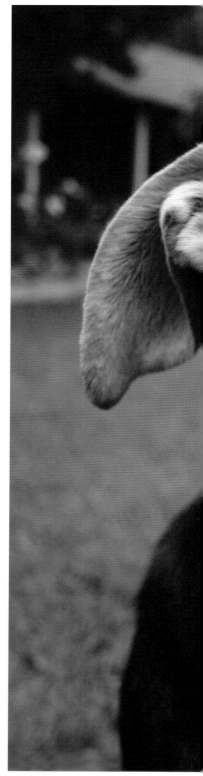

Maggie

ody, a six-year-old German shepherd, came from the pound as a puppy and impressed cofounder and grape-grower Ken Nerlove and his family right away. Smart and gracious, Cody could have been an excellent police or guide dog. When he was four, the family returned to the pound to find him a companion. While most of the dogs there were jumping and barking in their cages, one mutt—who shared a cage with a German shepherd—simply gazed at them, watching silently yet turning away whenever they looked at her. They left that day but couldn't stop thinking about the skinny, odd-looking dog who was so shy. When they brought her home, however, the eleven-month-old Maggie romped through the yard and dunked her entire head in the water bowl. Today, at age three, Maggie is still full of energy, leading Cody in her capers—stealing food in the kitchen and chasing the cat. The Nerlove family knows that while they are at work at the winery, the patient, calm Cody and the adventurous Maggie are perfect companions.

Bubba

OTIS & BUBBA
ELYSE WINERY

Otis

Otis, a seven-year-old German shorthair, and Bubba, a three-year-old boxer, are teacher and student, respectively. When winemaker Mike Trotta began working with winery owners Ray and Nancy Coursen, he brought the puppy Bubba with him. Otis immediately found the perfect student and taught Bubba to point—and now the winery has two expert squirrel dogs. Otis also taught Bubba to keep pace with visitors to guide them to the tasting room. During harvest, Bubba learned the tasting techniques quickly. Like Ray, who continually searches for "the most wonderful fruit" for his wine, Otis and Bubba can't keep away from the best-tasting specimens. According to Nancy, the two easily eat their weight in grapes.

JET
FRAZIER WINERY

Jet, an eight-year-old golden retriever mix—fathered by an unknown black dog around the corner—is vineyard manager Jon Frazier's steadfast companion and morale booster. In the vineyards, Jet is crucial to keeping the workers' spirits high day by day, whether he's giving them affection or entertaining them with his antics. One day, as Jet chased a rabbit, the rabbit raced up a worker's body and used his head as a springboard, leaping away from Jet and making everyone laugh. Another day Jet somehow got into the adjacent golf course, and an amused golfer lifted Jet over the high fence to return him to Jon. Jet has also visited retirement communities, where the residents love to pet and feed him. "There's something spiritual about what Jet brings to us," Jon says. "On the most difficult days, this job would be terrible without my dog."

EDNA
KIRKLAND RANCH WINERY

Edna, a seven-month-old Scottish terrier, is content inside the winery. As Debi Kirkland, the director of administration, says, Edna "sits pretty," demurely back on two legs, and she speaks nicely on command. Often planting herself behind the register, she knows how to get attention. But her truly original talent shines outdoors. Like the five generations of the Kirkland family who operate the ranch, Edna knows how to work the land. When Debi shows her a weed, she sniffs it thoughtfully, and then she finds others like it and pulls them up. Occasionally she's distracted by butterflies, but of course she's too young to work all day.

Jake

BABU & JAKE
MONTICELLO VINEYARDS

Babu, age thirteen, and Jake, age four, might first appear to be unassuming black Labrador retrievers wandering about Chris Corley's property. But as visitors find out, often too late, the dogs are masters in the art of the hard sell. On tours, the Labs greet visitors warmly, and Babu sometimes takes someone's hand in his mouth to show the way. Jake impresses guests with his running speed and adept swimming—and he even opens the doors to the winery. But once visitors are in the tasting room, the shrewd marketing techniques begin. Babu sits on someone's feet and refuses to budge. Then Gayle Klokow from hospitality informs the imprisoned taster, "Only after you make a purchase will Babu get off your feet." And lest others try to exit too soon, Jake blocks the tasting-room door with his impressive weight, encouraging more sales. As guests leave with their excellent purchases, Babu and Jake—always appreciative—nuzzle up against them as if nothing ever happened.

Babu (front) &
Jake

Syrah

SYRAH & MINNIE
Van Der Heyden Vineyards

The Van Der Heyden property is home to nearly twenty cats because, as office manager Andrea Gregg says, "people keep dropping them off here." That's why Minnie, a twelve-year-old Australian shepherd/German shepherd mix, is so important—she chases and plays with the cats whenever she can. During the winery's tasting hours, Minnie is accepting of all guests and children, but before 10 a.m. and after 6 p.m., she guards the house and barks at anyone who approaches. Her canine cohort, Chateau Petite Syrah De Vine, is a one-year-old Australian shepherd who follows Andrea everywhere. Indulgent of small children who grab her neck and wrestle her to the ground, Syrah loves all people and never gets tired of dog treats and sweet grapes. In their own ways, Minnie and Syrah ensure that the Gregg family, the winery's guests, and the growing population of cats are never lonely.

Minnie

SALLY
WILLIAM HILL WINERY

Sally, an eight-year-old yellow Labrador retriever, was found cold and shivering under a bridge during a storm in 1998. Today she is warm and cheerful, running freely along the Silverado Bench. Chief viticulturist and vineyard manager Tony Fernandez Jr. and operations administrator Dana Estensen say that Sally is such good company that sometimes one of the maintenance workers takes her home after work. Because Sally's favorite place is the laboratory, Tony and Dana think of her as a laboratory researcher, but at times she races from door to door at the winery until someone lets her in with open arms. With one paw always in the air while she sits, Sally is continually reaching out in friendship.

Oakville

Gargiulo Vineyards

Groth Vineyards & Winery

Miner Family Vineyards

Oakville Ranch Vineyards

Plumpjack Winery

Rudd Vineyards & Winery

Saddleback Cellars

LILY
GARGIULO VINEYARDS

Inspecting gardens is an arduous task, as Lily—the seven-year-old Maltese—knows well. She carefully examines each garden, nosing her way between bushes and sniffing every flower and herb, and she chases gophers down into their holes. Only the sound of tires on the gravel driveway can set her running to the winery. Visitors fall in love with her immediately and threaten to steal her on the way out. Some guests even send her home-baked treats and handmade clothes. But as soon as the guests leave—without Lily, as the Gargiulo family ensures—she hurries back to the gardens. By the end of the day, her white hair is filled with rosemary, sage, and vineyard dust.

China Moon

Chow Fun

CHINA MOON, JOY LUCK & CHOW FUN
GROTH VINEYARDS & WINERY

China Moon (age fifteen), Frank Fat (age thirteen, not pictured), Joy Luck (age four), and Chow Fun (age four) were named after the Chinese restaurants that Dennis and Judy Groth love the most. The bold pugs have created havoc by snatching toys, pacifiers, and food from small children—and they've even chewed on tasters' beautiful sandals at the bar. The Groths' dearly departed pug Tommy Toy once interrupted a large business meeting for winery owners by grabbing a wallet from a purse and retreating to a corner for a good chew. "Pugs have a great sense of humor," says Judy, "and they amuse us all day long."

Joy Luck (front) & China Moon

ELLA
MINER FAMILY VINEYARDS

Ella, a six-year-old springer spaniel, is an office dog most days. She loves customers, children, other dogs, and even cats. To showcase Ella's ability to please, French artist Jean-Pierre Got is creating a fanciful poster of Ella serving wine to owner Emily Miner at a bistro table. To Dave Miner's dismay, when Ella hits the vineyards, all her good graces are forgotten. She'll chase lizards for hours and hours until she reluctantly obeys Dave's whistle. A shameless beggar, she has to be kept away from picnickers. At an employee barbeque one year, everyone laughed as Ella snuck away from an employee's plate with a large rib in her mouth.

Winery Dogs of Napa Valley

ROMEO
OAKVILLE RANCH VINEYARDS

Romeo, a four-year-old bull mastiff, has proved he can be as dramatic as his Shakespearean namesake. A fine greeter and "ambassadog," Romeo loves to watch a particular cat that lingers on the property. One day he ventured to the cat's favorite part of the vineyards. To the horror of general manager Paula Kornell, he came back dragging the back half of his body—convincing her he'd been attacked by a snake. Upon closer inspection, however, it was clear that Romeo had simply suffered a minor cat scratch and was hoping for some excitement and sympathy.

Hallie

HALLIE & REGGIE
PLUMPJACK WINERY

Hallie and Reggie know how to please a crowd. Hallie, a six-year-old English springer spaniel, is so popular that John Conover, the winery's general manager, gets frequent letters and e-mails from starstruck visitors asking about her. Reggie, also known as Sir Reginald's Rip Tide, is a two-year-old black Labrador retriever with a similar gift of celebrity. As winemaker Tony Biagi says, Reggie is known as the resident "rock star" because visitors get excited when he's around. Fortunately, Hallie and Reggie both know how to take a break from their admirers. Hallie eats Cabernet Sauvignon grapes until she's full, finds a nice spot in the sun for napping, and grins—John says—as the grapes ferment in her stomach. Reggie cools down in the pond, swimming quietly in his solitude until he hears the call of the winery's restless crowd.

Reggie

TESS
RUDD VINEYARDS & WINERY

Tess, a three-year-old Bernese mountain dog, is the winery's official greeter. When winery owner Leslie Rudd arrives at the office each day, Tess is beside him. At the hospitality office, she receives her first biscuit of the day from her own cookie jar, and then she greets the staff one by one. Without fail, she finds her place at the front door to welcome every visitor. "Tess makes the entire experience here at Rudd feel approachable," says winery owner Susan Rudd. "Since Tess is such a gentle, friendly, and easygoing creature, she lets guests know immediately that they are welcome."

PAYTON & RILEY
SADDLEBACK CELLARS

Riley & Payton

Payton, a two-year-old yellow Labrador retriever, and Riley, a black Labrador retriever a few months younger, are good friends. But when Riley was adopted from a shelter last April, Payton—the usually mellow, cuddly "old soul"—needed to show Riley she was boss. For two weeks, the two dogs resembled a tornado with their wrestling, but now it's clear she won: whenever Riley has a bone that Payton wants, Riley concedes, dropping the bone. Still, says assistant winemaker Jeff Fontanella, they both love running in the vineyards—Payton tasting the tips of grapes and Riley herding up squirrels and rabbits. At harvest, Payton rolls around in the discarded grape skins, coming home pink. It's anyone's guess what Riley the runner will get into this year.

Rutherford

Grgich Hills Cellar

Honig Vineyard & Winery

Provenance Vineyards

Quintessa

Sequoia Grove Vineyards and Winery

Staglin Family Vineyard

Sullivan Vineyards

Trahan Winery

POSIP
GRGICH HILLS CELLAR

Posip, a seven-year-old Australian shepherd/Border collie mix, was named for the white wine that owner and winemaker Mike Grgich makes in Croatia. Maryanne Wedner, Mike's longtime assistant, picked Posip from her hairstylist's dog's litter to give Mike the perfect canine companion. Posip loved Mike right away, understanding his English and Croatian commands in no time. Today, after running freely in the vineyards, Posip greets visitors in the parking lot and licks their hands in the tasting room—instantly infusing happiness even before the guests taste the wine.

Sadie

BUZZ & SADIE
HONIG VINEYARD & WINERY

Buzz, Henri, and Sadie—a trio of professionals—have divided up their duties at the winery. Buzz, a one-year-old Labrador retriever, entertains the children who visit. Playful and patient, he was everything the Honigs were hoping for when they won him at a Tulsa charity auction. Henri (not pictured), an eleven-year-old puli, works the parties. Interacting with guests, she is never surprised when someone "accidentally" drops a delicious hors d'oeuvre on the floor. Sadie, an eleven-year-old Border collie, accompanies salesperson Jennifer Kopp everywhere. She therefore goes to the office, to the stable, to meetings, and to parties. "In a stern, loving way," says Elaine Honig, "Sadie keeps us all together, safe and organized."

Buzz

GYPSY
PROVENANCE VINEYARDS

Gypsy Rain Rutherford Dust, a seven-month-old toy poodle, is in training to be a winery dog. When she comes to the office, she sleeps with one eye open, waiting to dance at the sight of a new face. When it's time to play, Gypsy bounces down the stairs like a ballerina, silently springing across the smooth floor of the tasting room and weaving in and out of the assemblage of legs, handbags, and any hand reaching down to pet her. Named for the taste that the earth gives to the wine, Gypsy loves the Rutherford dust outside. Hopping in the front lawn, with her apricot fur gleaming in the sunlight, she has already started entertaining visitors. "Gypsy has a way of softening everyone's mood," say winemaker Tom Rinaldi and his daughter Angelina. "She lifts our spirits and adds joy and motivation, especially on Mondays!"

SAMMY
QUINTESSA

Sammy, a seven-year-old mutt (possibly part Labrador retriever and part Dalmatian), came to winemaker Aaron Pott from a life spent indoors with a Hollywood director. Though the director said that Sammy hated water, the first thing Sammy did at the biodynamic vineyard was leap joyfully into the irrigation lake. At the sorting table, Sammy eats not only the rejected grapes but also the yellow jackets that bother everyone. Inside the tasting room, he'll put his head on any taster's lap in a plea for cheese, something he can't get enough of. When he sits, Sammy looks like a "sausage with four toothpicks," Aaron says, but when he runs, he looks positively heroic. When Nicolas Joly, the French ersatz patron saint of biodynamics, first saw Sammy running with abandon through the vineyard, he exclaimed, *"That dog is biodynamique!"*

Sarah (front),
Dizzy (left) & Dusty

DIZZY, DUSTY & SARAH
SEQUOIA GROVE VINEYARDS AND WINERY

Dusty, a twelve-year-old black Labrador mix, is a loyal friend, waiting in the driveway for vineyardist Steve Allen to come home. Dizzy, a two-year-old Australian shepherd mix, is just as loyal, waiting with Dusty in the driveway. But Sarah, Dizzy's sister, is the wild one—she's been clocked running 36 mph beside Steve's motorcycle. She's also the one who likes skunks, but the skunks don't feel the same way, as any winery employee with a nose has discovered. Luckily, Sarah enjoys swimming wherever she finds water on the Rutherford Bench, so she can join Steve, Dusty, and Dizzy at the winemaker dinners, parties, and film festivals at Sequoia Grove.

Dusty (front) & Dizzy

KARA
STAGLIN FAMILY VINEYARD

Garen and Shari Staglin have traditionally had Jack Russell terriers at their winery. The Staglins' driveway is even flanked by two pillars featuring Jack Russell terriers on top. Two of their Jack Russells, Deuce and Sami, entertained cast and crew at the filming of Disney's 1997 remake of *The Parent Trap*, a film that featured the Staglins' villa and vineyards in many scenes. When coyotes became a problem at the vineyard, Garen and Shari got Kara, now a two-year-old Anatolian shepherd, as a guard dog. Each morning and late each afternoon, Kara surveys the vineyard on her walks with the Staglins. When she sees rabbits, turkeys, or deer, she darts off into the rows to chase them from the fruit. Between her patrols, she wades contentedly in the long, beautiful pool or rests in her own corral under a big oak tree. A loyal companion with a spirit of independence and a love of the land, Kara is clearly thriving at the Staglin home.

Boe

BOE & ZSA ZSA
SULLIVAN VINEYARDS

Zsa Zsa

"Balls just fall from the sky at Sullivan Vineyards," says Kelleen Sullivan. Boe, a fourteen-year-old yellow Labrador retriever, and Zsa Zsa, a six-year-old golden retriever, can't keep away from the Ball Tree. To the Sullivans, it's just an apple tree that has been pruned low to the ground, but to Boe and Zsa Zsa, it's an endless supply of balls. Every day they pick balls from the tree and toss them to anyone who will toss them back. After a few rounds, the balls suddenly become apples, and the two eat them as snacks. When visitors arrive, Boe leads them to the tasting room and lies on the cool floor while they sip wine. Zsa Zsa, who loves to keep playing, leads visitors to the pond, hoping they'll throw balls out into the water for her to fetch.

SADIE
TRAHAN WINERY

When winemaker Chuck Custodio and his wife, Janna, stopped by the pound one day, they asked which dog was the next to be put down. Next in line was Sadie, a four-year-old German shorthaired pointer who was picked up off the street with no collar and a tennis ball in her mouth. According to Chuck, in the last five years she hasn't dropped the ball since. When guests with children visit the winery, Sadie gives them a relaxing experience. The parents can take their time to drink wine while their kids throw the ball (or wine barrel bung) for Sadie, as far and as often as they can, laughing as they watch the "crazy running dog" go after it. A fiercely dependable presence, Sadie is the Cal Ripken, Jr. of the winery business, bringing happiness to everyone she sees every day.

Spring Mountain

Behrens & Hitchcock

Cain Vineyard & Winery

Domaine Charbay Winery & Distillery

Guilliams Winery

Robert Keenan Winery

Schweiger Vineyards

Stony Hill Vineyard

Chien
Lunatique

LUCY
BEHRENS & HITCHCOCK

Lucy, a seven-year-old Jack Russell terrier, is a daring individualist. At a young age, she was hit by a Ford 150, an ATV, and a motorcycle. When her pelvis was broken, she surprised everyone with her strong recovery. Today no one would know that she almost didn't make it. Though Jack Russell terriers are known for disliking water, Lucy spends countless hours at home splashing around in the swimming pool. Equally vivacious at work, she opens the heavy wooden winery doors with her teeth—evidenced by the bite marks in the wood—to chase lizards and mice in the vineyards. Winery owners Les Behrens and Lisa Drinkward, in awe of Lucy's energy and tenacity, have named a Syrah for her, Chien Lunatique.

Winery Dogs of Napa Valley

ROBO
CAIN VINEYARD & WINERY

Robo, a five-year-old rottweiler mix, is a true vineyard dog. With no single owner, he belongs to the vineyard crew, riding in the back of the pickup truck and bathing in the strong sunlight above the fog on Spring Mountain. He barely lifts his head when a rabbit hops by, and he tires out quickly when pursuing a deer. Instead, he prefers the camaraderie of the crew—and the burritos they share with him. Sometimes it seems Robo forgets he's a dog. One day, vineyard supervisor Gustavo De Haro led Robo to the garage to feed him. As Gustavo lifted the bag of dog food, a mouse ran out. One of Gustavo's colleagues in the barn screamed and jumped up on the counter. Robo, equally upset, ran outside and jumped up on the picnic table. Gustavo couldn't stop laughing at the gigantic dog who was afraid of such a tiny mouse.

Snifter

SUNNY & SNIFTER
DOMAINE CHARBAY WINERY & DISTILLERY

Sunny

Sunny and Snifter love to be near people—greeting them, walking alongside them, and making them happy. Sunny, a six-year-old Australian shepherd/tick coon hound mix, runs to welcome visitors and kiss them over and over. Snifter, also known as "Sniffy," is a two-year-old Jack Russell terrier who pokes his nose into guests' cars to get a whiff—and maybe a taste—of their delicious snacks and pastries. But as much as they love every visitor, they are most attached to Susan and Miles Karakasevic. At the end of the day, they lead the winery owners home, pausing at the gardens as Susan and Miles pick tomatoes for dinner. At home, Sunny settles down comfortably while Snifter falls deeply asleep on Miles' lap.

ANGIE
GUILLIAMS VINEYARDS

Angie, a nine-year-old black Labrador retriever, sleeps for much of the day in the azalea bushes, getting up occasionally to roll in the dirt or snow. At night she hunts in the vineyards, catching moles and getting sprayed by skunks. But her goal is clearly to meet a fox. Litters of foxes are born in the drain system, and workers can see the kits leaping up into the air and down into their holes by day. At night the foxes' cries can be heard a quarter of a mile away, and the sounds of their scurrying echo in the pipes. Angie waits for hours at different pipe openings, alert for the moment a fox will appear. As far as owner and winemaker John Guilliams knows, Angie has yet to see a fox. But as long as she wants to lie at the pipe openings at night, she'll always have a restful place to sleep in the day.

Scrappy (front) & Scooby

SCOOBY & SCRAPPY
ROBERT KEENAN WINERY

Scrappy, a two-year-old black Labrador retriever mix, is a "big ham," says Laura Kewell, tasting-room manager and special-events coordinator. He loves attention, and he knows that visitors can't resist him when he runs to the parking lot to meet them. After leading them into the cool, dark tasting room, he tries hard to lie against everyone's feet at the bar. A true "mama's dog," he doesn't like to venture off alone. If Laura leads him down into the cellar of French and American oak barrels, he'll pull the barrel chalks and chew on them contentedly. Scooby, an eleven-year-old mutt who does not have Scrappy's social graces, tends to bark genially at visitors rather than greet them. But he has no trouble finding happiness any day of the week. He snacks on dried figs scattered on the property, rides with abandon on the work truck, and to the entertainment of anyone watching, slides down the winery's grassy hill on his back, over and over again, until he's hungry for more figs.

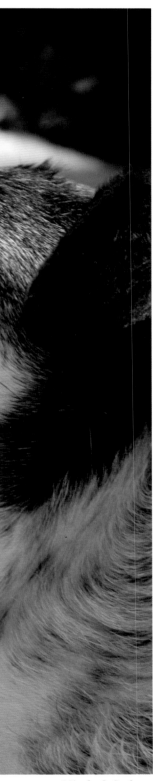

Mindy & Sydney

Blitzen

SYDNEY, BLITZEN & MINDY
SCHWEIGER VINEYARDS

Anyone who first meets Sydney, a yellow Labrador retriever, and her daughter Blitzen, fathered by a stealthy Border collie named X, must think they lead a carefree life. While Sydney greets visitors with a leaf, stick, or fir cone in her mouth, Blitzen shows off her skills bouncing a beach ball from her nose. Sydney tastes the ripe grapes, Blitzen follows Fred Schweiger everywhere, and they both rest well when tired, in the comfort of the winery office. But then Mindy, a fifteen-year-old beagle/terrier mix, arrives. Although she has officially retired to the back office, she'll appear unexpectedly to harass Sydney and Blitzen, nipping at their legs as her own parents on the cattle ranch must have taught her. An excellent nurse, Mindy licks Sydney and Blitzen's ears, curing infections, and the two younger dogs give her kisses in return.

Katie Scarlet

KATIE SCARLET & LUCIANO
STONY HILL VINEYARD

Luciano, a five-year-old yellow Labrador retriever, was named after the bloodthirsty gangster "Lucky" Luciano. Fortunately, Luciano the Lab is mellow, calmly vacuuming Chardonnay grapes from the ground when employees are crushing. Longtime winemaker Mike Chelini, who loves all things Italian, still thinks the name fits—especially when he asks, in a heavy Italian accent, "Hey, Luch, how 'bout a glass of wine?" Luciano usually defers, preferring instead to follow Mike wherever he goes, even if Mike is speeding away on his Honda Foreman. Katie Scarlet, a gentle eight-year-old Brittany spaniel, was named after Scarlet O'Hara. Unlike the fictional character, though, Katie Scarlet—whose father was a champion show dog—is shy with strangers and doesn't care for men. With her excellent nose, she sniffs for hours alone in the vineyard, enjoying the quiet open spaces. She rests under proprietor Willenda McCrea's desk, a soothing, heartfelt companion and a peaceful presence.

Luciano

St. Helena

Anomaly Vineyards

Arger - Martucci Vineyards

Arietta

Broman Cellars

Buehler Vineyards

Chappellet Vineyard and Winery

Chateau Boswell Winery

Clark - Claudon Vineyards

Corison Winery

Ehlers Estate

Kelham Vineyards

Kuleto Estate Family Vineyards

Livingston Moffett Winery

Rombauer Vineyards

RustRidge Ranch and Winery

Salvestrin Estate Vineyard and Winery

S.E. Chase Family Cellars

Spottswoode Estate Vineyard & Winery

TOR Wines/Kenward Family Vineyards

V. Sattui Winery

Varozza Vineyards

Venge Vineyards

Whitehall Lane Winery

Cosette

ASHBY & COSETTE
ANOMALY VINEYARDS

Thanks to winery owners Linda and Steve Goldfarb, Anomaly Vineyards is never without the love of a good dog—or two. Years ago, the winery was ruled by Indee, a loving husky/shepherd mix whose image is on Anomaly's label. Today, in Indee's Vineyard, an eleven-year-old Jack Russell terrier mix named Ashby shares the run of the property with his older companion, Cosette, a nurturing poodle mix. As a puppy, Ashby was lucky that Linda happened to be driving by him at the right time. At the side of the road a young woman was holding Ashby in the air, waving him around to attract attention. When Linda stopped, the woman said Ashby needed a new home immediately. The Goldfarbs didn't need a new dog—they were all content with Indee—but Ashby's leg was badly fractured and Linda knew the puppy needed a chance. Today, despite a foot that turns slightly outward, Ashby is healthy and happy. Cosette, who was rescued on the streets of St. Helena, is his best friend and protector, keeping an eye on him every day.

Ashby

Sable

Kallisto

SABLE & KALLISTO
ARGER - MARTUCCI VINEYARDS

Sable, an eight-year-old French Brittany spaniel, is a graceful presence in the tasting room. Nicknamed "Lady" because she crosses her front paws when she sits, she's a sweet "mama's girl," says Katarena Arger, director of sales and marketing and tasting room manager. The daughter of two of Katarena's previous Brittany spaniels, Sable soars through the vineyards, ducking lithely between the vines. Muddy and refreshed, she returns to Katarena, dropping rodents silently at her feet. Kallisto, a six-month-old Brittany spaniel, is known as "Kalliper the Galloper" because she runs like a horse. When she's not chasing flies and mice, she's attending wine events at Katarena's side and learning the business.

OLIVER
ARIETTA

Oliver, a five-year-old Bernese mountain dog, was not the medium-sized companion that Arietta winery owner Fritz Hatton was hoping for. But Caren Hatton had already met a Bernese puppy in San Francisco, so no other breed would do. Born in Gilroy, Oliver won Fritz and Caren's hearts right away and showed his unconditional love for children when Libby and Hattie were born. Today Oliver is good for business, helping to keep Arietta in the public eye. In fact, he's a magnet whenever he's strolling with the family in St. Helena—at least ten people each day stop to pet him, and some of the store owners have treats ready for his arrival.

Brandy

BRANDY AND BOOMER
BROMAN CELLARS

B ob and Deborah Russell Broman found their two perfect canine companions at the Humane Society of Napa County. Boomer, a five-year-old Labrador retriever, impressed the Bromans immediately with his gentle disposition. Brandy, a five-year-old Labrador retriever/shepherd mix, came to them with fleas, heartworm, and an unhappy past. Though she had run away from two previous homes, she fit right in with Boomer and the family's cats, Squeaks and Diva. Today the dogs and cats go for long walks together in the vineyard, taking breaks so that Diva can groom the dogs. When guests arrive, Boomer and Brandy are the first to welcome them. "There's nothing like a wagging tail and a happy face," says Deborah, "to make anyone's day brighter."

Boomer

Coco

PORTO & COCO
BUEHLER VINEYARDS

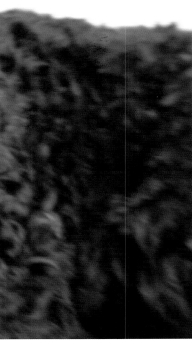

Porto and Coco are kitchen dogs, and neither likes to stray too far from the enticing scents. Porto, a ten-year-old Portuguese water dog, is an excellent greeter and guard dog with a talent for putting visitors at ease. Occasionally, when he's had his fill of food, he leads the household's toy poodles—Smokey, Bandit, and Reba (not pictured)—to the pond, and they all return home wet and filthy. Coco, on the other hand, never gets tired of eating. An eight-month-old miniature Shih Tzu, Coco insists on tasting all food—even radishes and bananas—before it is served to anyone. According to John and Lisa Buehler, her love of anything edible means she has "quickly exceeded her genetic potential in weight." But she's not content to wait for food all day. When there's a pause in serving, she'll throw a ball for herself and run to fetch it, never failing to make the Buehlers and their guests laugh.

Porto

OMAR
CHAPPELLET VINEYARD & WINERY

In some ways, Omar, a seven-year-old Anatolian Shepherd, behaves the way he is expected to. At 160 pounds, he is intimidating in size and temperament, protective of his family and the property. Anatolians were bred to guard goats and sheep in Turkey, and Omar—in an odd twist—has adopted winery owner Cyril Chappellet as his "flock," both protecting and respecting him. Proudly sporting a dog tag that reads "Canine Sommelier," from Blakesley Chappellet's Dogs Uncorked line of dog products, Omar is an essential part of the winery. In his domain on Pritchard Hill, he's content to keep Cyril company in the office, ride shotgun in the 1960 customized Land Cruiser used for winery tours, or sit on the porch to welcome visitors. Those who know Omar best are humored by his unique way of showing affection, vigorously nuzzling their heads and necks.

Jackson

JOHN ROBIE & JACKSON
CHATEAU BOSWELL WINERY

John Robie, a three-year-old golden retriever, was named after the jewel burglar played by Cary Grant in *To Catch a Thief*. "Although he is handsome, he's not sly," says winery owner Susan Boswell, thanks in part to his excellent dog training by Brandt Wilson of Top Dawgs. He is generally well-behaved—treading carefully through the obsidian, volcanic ash, and numerous Indian arrowheads on the property and eventually coming home relatively calm and clean. But when his favorite visitor, Jackson—Jacquelynn and Josh Peeples' very persuasive eight-year-old black Labrador retriever—leads him to the pond to swim, the dogs won't come out until they're dragged out. And of course both emerge covered in green slime, refreshed and happy to shake themselves dry and move on to the next adventure.

MIA
CLARK - CLAUDON VINEYARDS

Mia, a five-year-old black Labrador retriever, has three loves: she loves vineyard owner Tom Clark, she loves to play, and she loves to eat. As vineyard owner Laurie Claudon knows, if Mia is left at home while Tom goes to the vineyards, she howls all day, so Mia has a dog bed on Tom's Honda four-wheeler. And despite the metal plate in her front right leg, Mia loves to play for hours in the creek and the vineyard, chasing lizards and frogs. She eats ripe grapes and steals workers' lunches, and one day she mistakenly thought Tom was playing with her and feeding her at the same time. When Tom cleaned out the sand filter, he tossed out shovelsful of fine silica sand, not realizing Mia was catching and eating it. She ate nearly eight pounds of sand that day, Tom estimated, and was sick for the next two days. Now, knowing her appetite, Tom and the vineyard crew all keep an eye on Mia.

Puck

PUCK & EMMA
CORISON WINERY

A happy pair, Puck and Emma fit right in at the winery. Cathy Corison has lived with dogs at her winery for thirty years, and she can't imagine her life—whether she's creating wine at her gray barn or enjoying her family at home—without dogs by her side. Puck, a three-year-old collie, was bred to herd and is therefore talented at keeping the family together. Emma, a six-month-old Bernese mountain dog, has been to obedience school but is still in training to be a winery dog. One day soon Puck and Emma will roam together in the vineyards and come running when they hear Cathy or her husband, William Martin, calling them. Already they love the rewards of affection whenever they see family, friends, and visitors.

Puck & Emma

RIPLEY
EHLERS ESTATE

Ripley, a six-year-old Australian shepherd, is a big-hearted dog with an even bigger appetite. As soon as he arrives at the winery each day with winemaker Rudy Zuidema, he makes his rounds, checking in with everyone at the office and hoping for a treat. At 9:45 a.m., he heads to the vineyard to share a taco with the crew. Ripley's inner clock tells him when every employee takes a break, so no one is surprised when he shows up for a snack. Always grateful, Ripley thanks everyone by jumping up to kiss their faces.

Skip (front) &
Gabby

134

GABBY, SKIP & PEACHES
KELHAM VINEYARDS

Peaches

Gabby, Skip, and Peaches get along famously, but they couldn't be more different. Gabby, a one-year-old black Labrador retriever, the runt of the litter, appears to have "nipple anxiety," say winery owners Rawson and Susanna Kelham, because she always has something in her mouth. Skip, the six-year-old Jack Russell "terrorist," runs and makes a racket, getting everyone riled up before he trots home. He never gets in trouble, though, and his attention-getting techniques have even won him a place on an upcoming wine label. Peaches, a regal nine-year-old Rhodesian Ridgeback with multiple sclerosis, functions as the winery's queen. She is a commanding presence on the deck, saturating herself in the morning sun. As the day wears on, she assumes her position on her throne. From there she monitors the platters of food as they're delivered from the kitchen to the tasters, silently emanating her royal approval.

Pilot

PILOT & PANCHITA
KULETO ESTATE FAMILY VINEYARDS

Full of boundless energy, Pilot and Panchita greet new visitors like old friends. Panchita, a five-year-old black Labrador retriever/Border collie mix, is the estate's tour guide. When she's not running in circles around guests, she's awing them with her water ballet routine, a complicated sequence involving hoses and spouts in the swimming pool. Loyal to a fault, Panchita follows Pat Kuleto's Pathfinder around the estate. One day a member of the winery team borrowed it and didn't notice Panchita following him until he reached St. Helena—fourteen miles away. Pilot, an eight-month-old chocolate Labrador, is the estate's greeter, goodwill ambassador, and occasional wedding-cake eater. His choice of cuisine—from dead mice to bloated frogs and even glass—has astounded and at times terrified the family. An able swimmer and a duck hunter in training, Pilot is beloved by all, especially Pat's son, Daniel.

Panchita

Whiskey & Patty

PATTY & WHISKEY
LIVINGSTON MOFFETT WINERY

Patty and Whiskey, both seven-year-old Australian shepherds, are fearless hunters. They spend most of their hours tracking animal scents and return home dragging deer heads and squirrel carcasses. One day Patty chased a deer over the hill behind the winery and returned, breathless and happy, with a deep puncture wound in her chest, clearly the loser in a good fight. When the hunters are at home, winery owner John Livingston enjoys playing ball with Whiskey while Patty rests comfortably. Both dogs get along so well with guests and the winery's three cats that the casual observer would never suspect their unquenchable passion for the hunt.

Whiskey

Winery Dogs of Napa Valley

Moose Rombauer
Winery Greeter

TELEPHONE 707-963-5170   WINE ORDERS 800-622-2206
FACSIMILE 707-963-5752   www.rombauervineyards.com
3522 Silverado Trail · St. Helena · California 94574

MOOSE
ROMBAUER VINEYARDS

Moose, a four-year-old chocolate Labrador retriever, is a gentle soul, spending most of his time strolling through the wooded property, socializing in the tasting room, and napping in the office. One day, when a summer employee brought orphaned young kittens to the office to bottle-feed them during her breaks, the 100-pound Moose sauntered over and licked one of the kittens lovingly, even though the 4.3-ounce kitten was the size of Moose's nose. Winery owners Koerner and Joan Rombauer adopted Moose three years ago from a military couple who had to ship out just before the war. Another couple adopted Moose's brother, Travis. Recently, Moose and Travis were reunited for a visit. When they met again, at last, their hair stood on end and they circled each other for a while. Then something clicked and they became ecstatic, jumping and yelping. The Rombauers had never seen Moose so excited!

Tosca

TOSCA & CHARLIE
RustRidge Ranch and Winery

Tosca and Charlie—yellow Labrador retrievers, ages six and five—are mother and son. They are RustRidge's celebrities, having been featured in the *San Francisco Chronicle*, *Bark* magazine, and two 2005 yellow Labrador retriever calendars. Yet their fame has not gone to their heads. Each day they greet guests and escort them down the long, winding driveway to the tasting room. They also herd the ranch horses to the fence so that visitors can pet them. When they sense that visitors are about to enjoy a picnic lunch, Tosca and Charlie quickly move under the picnic tables, politely waiting for anything that might come their way. Sometimes a ranch cat also drops by to check out the offerings. Winery owners Jim Fresquez and Susan Meyer encourage Tosca and Charlie to lead their bed-and-breakfast's guests on hikes through the vineyards and hills. In the evenings, Tosca and Charlie enjoy hanging out with the guests on the B&B's front porch—a fitting end to a great day on the ranch.

Charlie

CJ

Rusty

RUSTY, JACK & CJ
SALVESTRIN ESTATE VINEYARD AND WINERY

Rusty, Jack, and CJ constantly entertain the many members of the Salvestrin family and their guests. Rusty, a two-year-old golden retriever, and Jack, a two-year-old Jack Russell terrier, have been playing together since they arrived at the winery. Now they're teaching CJ, a three-month-old Jack Russell terrier, to chase rabbits in the vineyard. When guests arrive at the winery or historic bed-and-breakfast, the trio races to greet them. "Our dogs are part of our family," says Susanne Salvestrin. "At our family-owned winery, our dogs extend the warmth and hospitality we strive so hard to show our guests."

CJ & Jack

PLADO
S.E. CHASE FAMILY CELLARS

Plado, a thirteen-year-old black Labrador retriever, is known as a connoisseur today, but this wasn't always the case—he earned his name when, as a puppy, he ate black Play-Doh. He now loves to drink the S.E. Chase Family Cellars wines and has been caught sampling directly from the filter press, so winery owner Pam Simpson has christened him an official wine taster. Sometimes rabbits in the vineyards lure him from his tasting duties, pulling Plado far from home, but he always returns for another taste of his favorite wine.

Murphy

GUS & MURPHY
SPOTTSWOODE ESTATE VINEYARD & WINERY

Gus, a fifteen-year-old black Labrador retriever, appeared on winery owner Mary Novak's doorstep one day when he was about one year old. A friend had picked him up on the Silverado Trail and asked Mary to watch him until a permanent home could be found. Mary, who had two other dogs at the time, took one look at Gus and said to her kids, "I think we've got three dogs now." A competent tour guide, Gus is loved by guests and employees. Murphy, a one-year-old black Labrador retriever, is a more energetic tour guide who slyly leans against guests when he wants to be petted. He keeps Gus spry, nipping the older dog's ears when he wants to play. Together, Gus and Murphy chase cats and rabbits from the vineyard, earning their keep.

Gus

HONEY
TOR WINES
KENWARD FAMILY VINEYARDS

Honey, an eighteen-year-old golden retriever/cocker spaniel mix, came to Susan and Tor Kenward from another winemaker. For sixteen years, Honey has enjoyed her role as Kenward family dinner-party dog, sitting convivially at the feet of guests as they drink wine. Gentle and loving, she brings good feeling to the home—at one time she even slept regularly with the quirky family cat and two pet rabbits in the soft dog bed. A patient and sweet friend to all, she has inspired Molly, Tor and Susan's daughter, to study veterinary medicine.

Tessa (front)
& Elvis

Czor

TESSA, CZOR & ELVIS
V. SATTUI WINERY

Tessa and Czor, both age two, and Elvis, one, come from a German line of Bernese mountain dogs and serve as the winery's most visible ambassadors. President Tom Davies takes one each day to the office with him and gets stopped wherever he goes along the way—in the deli, in the tasting room, or on the picnic grounds. Tessa, who was chosen from the litter for her gregariousness, is always excited to meet hundreds of guests a day and to occasionally snatch a salami from someone's shopping basket. Czor, says Tom's wife, Cara Davies, is their quiet, easygoing "big boy" and prefers never to leave Tom's side. Elvis came to them with a heart defect, but since a valve was repaired in surgery, he's become energetic, hilarious, and excellent company for Tessa and Czor. Though Tom admires their marketing abilities, he rarely brings all three to work at once. If he does, he's sorry. "Their popularity makes it impossible to get office work done," he says, shaking his head.

Lupo

LUPO & LUCA
V. SATTUI WINERY

Lupo, a four-year-old longhaired German shepherd, has lived with Daryl Sattui, the winery owner, since he was seven weeks old. Therefore, Lupo—which means "wolf"—follows Daryl everywhere, and Daryl may even take him along on his next trip to Europe. Loyal, loving, and sensitive, Lupo gets along with the myriad dogs and guests on the grounds. Luca, a four-year-old Australian shepherd, understands three languages—English, Icelandic, and American Sign Language—and is learning Spanish from viticultural technician Jo Blank, who loves languages. Luca is a hard worker in the field, always following staff members around to make sure they're working. During the rainy season, he digs at the gopher holes and growls into them, helping the workers determine which runs are active. Once, when cows got into the vineyard, he loudly told the cows they were on the wrong side of the fence and he tried, with some success, to herd them back to their pasture. Back at the office, he takes time to relax. He positions himself in the middle of the floor, waiting for any employee to give him a quick belly rub.

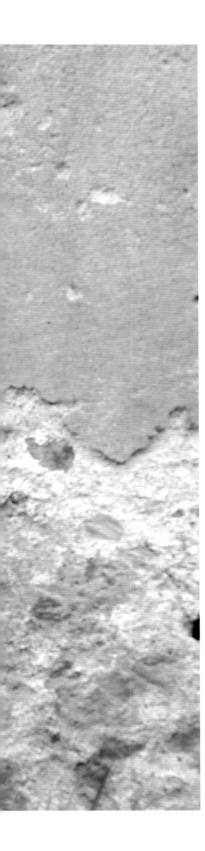

LUCY
VAROZZA VINEYARDS

Lucy, a one-year-old German shorthaired pointer, spends her days running. Rabbits don't have a chance to feast on the vines when Lucy's there, running and barking until they're gone. When the vineyard is free of intruders, she swims vigorously in the pond to cool down. All of this activity gives Lucy a voracious appetite, and winery owners Jack, Dianna, and Jason Varozza have learned the hard way that her appetite has no bounds. As a puppy, she grabbed a prime rib off the counter and pranced proudly into the living room to show off the giant piece of meat in her mouth. Months later, Dianna roasted a large chicken and left briefly to answer the phone. When she returned, Lucy had the chicken in her mouth—but she wasn't eating it. She was crying because she had just eaten her dinner and was too full for the chicken. These days, Lucy likes to find a spot at home where she can keep an eye on every member of the family—probably for the food opportunities, Dianna says.

LUCY
VENGE VINEYARDS

Lucy, a one-year-old golden retriever, was a welcome wedding present for Kirk and Sarah Venge. A rattlesnake bit Lucy when she was only seven weeks old, but she suffered no lasting damage. Though still young, Lucy is already known as an accomplished entertainer, making guests smile as she engages them during tours and tastings. Her stage presence increases when three creative girls at the winery dress her as a ballerina. As winery owners Nils and Kirk Venge know, if Lucy doesn't make it on Broadway, she will continue to dazzle her audience at Venge Vineyards.

Trigger

TIMBER & TRIGGER
WHITEHALL LANE WINERY

At ten years old, Timber — a yellow Labrador retriever — is just as hyper as she was at age two, says Tony Leonardini, retail sales manager. She's affectionate with everyone (except delivery men or those with facial hair), and regular visitors often arrive with the same two words: "Where's Timber?" If she's nowhere in sight, she's usually traipsing through the vineyards, going after rabbits, birds, and frogs and snacking on moths and mosquitoes. Sometimes Tony suspects she dines at a "mysterious restaurant" in St. Helena because she returns hours later and lies down with a heavy thump, drooling and burping with satisfaction. Timber's distant cousin, eight-month-old Trigger, has the same love of adventure. As a young puppy, she took off running and got caught in a rat trap. Freshly healed, she started experimenting with unusual snack foods, including crayons and a sponge. Lately, she's turned to chasing anything that runs and has already caught two birds and a gopher. Tony can only imagine what the dogs' other relatives like to eat.

Stags Leap

Clos Du Val

Regusci Winery

Shafer Vineyards

Signorello Vineyards

Steltzner Vineyards

Yountville

Goosecross Cellars

Alfie

ROARK, MAX & ALFIE
CLOS DU VAL

It is not unusual for employees at Clos Du Val's administration building to enjoy the company of a coworker's friendly dog. Traci Seville-Sharp feels lucky that Roark, a seven-year-old golden retriever, feels at home at her workplace—he plays with anyone who walks by, runs up and down the stairs, and sleeps on the smooth tile floor. Irma Muniz is glad to bring along Max, a seven-year-old mutt who at times chases his own tail, entertaining employees as he circles for several minutes at a time at high speed. Rose Galanty brings Alfie, a one-year-old standard poodle, to the tasting room to entertain guests. Alfie makes such a lasting impression that visitors send cards and photos to let Rose know that Alfie helped make their trip a great experience. When it's time for fresh air, Roark, Max, and Alfie run around together in the vineyard, and Max is excited to have two more tails to chase.

From left: Roark, Max & Alfie

Andy (front) and Trixie

Haas & Scrappy

ANDY, TRIXIE, HAAS & SCRAPPY
REGUSCI WINERY

She's only two feet tall, but few would argue that Trixie, or "Princess," as she prefers to be called, presides over Regusci Winery with a keen eye and a benevolent paw. Her entourage includes three male dogs. Andy, also a Welsh Corgi, acts as sentry and protector, ensuring everyone's safety under his watch. Haas and Scrappy, four-year-old yellow Labrador retrievers, provide muscle for the big jobs: inspecting limousines and announcing new guests as they arrive. Together, Princess and her boys are the consummate canine hospitality team. As Will Rogers once said, "If there are no dogs in Heaven, then when I die I want to go where they went." Trixie, Andy, Haas, and Scrappy already believe they're in heaven.

Andy & Trixie

TUCKER
SHAFER VINEYARDS

Tucker, a six-year-old yellow Labrador retriever, is winery owner John Shafer's third Labrador. Jake, a black Lab, loved to swim, and Rocky, a yellow Lab, spent his old age showing the young Tucker around. Tucker's arrival at the winery is heralded in the timeline of important dates posted in the office—in 1998, it is proclaimed, "John brings new puppy Tucker to the office, where he joins John's phone conversations and eats the mail." Today Tucker leaves John's mail alone, barking at the delivery trucks, devouring grapes, and greeting visitors. There's a sculpture of a Labrador on the front step, but it's hard to look at it long when Tucker is clamoring to say hello.

BANDIT
SIGNORELLO VINEYARDS

Intelligent and driven, Bandit—an eight-year-old Brittany spaniel and champion show dog—almost never gets into trouble. Thanks to Pierre Birebent, the winemaker, Bandit understands English and French and is excellent with visitors and children. During the day Bandit often runs free in a fenced twenty-acre vineyard, checking vines one by one, chasing rabbits, and pointing to quail. An astute bird dog, he also hunts with Pierre, pointing and fetching reliably. One day, though, Bandit stunned Pierre with his single-mindedness. When Pierre shot a pheasant over the Sacramento River, Bandit dove in, as expected, to retrieve it. However, the current was especially strong that day, and the pheasant kept getting farther and farther from the spaniel's reach. Bandit continued his pursuit for a mile and more, with Pierre running beside the river and calling in vain for him to get out. In the end, Bandit—barely shaken—emerged with the fallen pheasant, never knowing that Pierre feared he'd be lost in the river forever.

Finder & Magnus

FINDER & MAGNUS
STELTZNER VINEYARDS

Finder, age thirteen, and his son Magnus, age six, are two black Labrador retrievers that love to accompany winery owner Dick Steltzner in the field. Each has his own spot in Dick's old Isuzu, and they ride companionably, quiet and alert, until they see a rabbit or turkey to chase. Magnus is always speedy, running as fast as the turkeys run, but Finder—who lost his front leg after an accident with two cars on Highway 29—can't keep up. Finder, however, is the superior hunting partner and grape tester. Dick knows that when Finder deems the Cabernet Sauvignon grapes ripe enough for eating, it must be time to start picking. At some point, Magnus will also chew on ripe grapes, thereby cementing Dick's resolve. In the early spring, hungry coyotes have sometimes mistaken fat Magnus for a slow rabbit and a potentially tasty lunch. Luckily, Dick has been nearby to intervene, sometimes discharging a firearm to protect his valuable turkey-chaser.

MAIDCHEN
GOOSECROSS CELLARS

A stunning Great Dane mix, Maidchen, whose name means "young woman," is thirteen years old. Winery owners Patt and Rey Gorsuch adopted her from a Great Dane rescue society seven years ago, and she took to the winery life immediately. She protects the vineyards by chasing rabbits, and she's never too busy to greet guests. Noble, gentle, and attentive, she is memorable to everyone who is lucky enough to meet her. During the strongest heat of the day, she sleeps peacefully under her favorite vine.

WINERY LISTING

Acacia Vineyard
2750 Las Amigas Road, Napa, CA 94559
(707) 226-9991
acacia.info@acaciavineyard.com
www.acaciawinery.com
Tasting by Appointment, Mon-Sat 10-4, Sun 12-4

Altamura Winery and Vineyards
1700 Wooden Valley Road, Napa Valley, CA 94558
(707) 253-2000
altamurawinery@aol.com
www.altamura.com
Tasting by Appointment, Mon-Fri 10-3

Anomaly Vineyards
P.O. Box 741, St. Helena, CA 94574
(707) 967-8448
info@anomalyvineyards.com
www.anomalyvineyards.com

Arger - Martucci Vineyards
1455 Inglewood Avenue, St. Helena, CA 94574
(707) 963-4334
katiarger@aol.com
Tasting by Appointment, Thu-Mon 10-4

Arietta
(707) 963-5918
info@ariettawine.com
www.ariettawine.com

Behrens & Hitchcock
PO Box 1127, Calistoga, CA 94515
info@behrensandhitchcock.com
www.behrensandhitchcock.com

Bouchaine Vineyards
1075 Buchli Station Road, Napa, CA 94559
(800) 654-WINE
info@bouchaine.com
www.bouchaine.com
Open Tasting, Daily 10:30-4

Broman Cellars
945 Deer Park Road, St. Helena, CA 94574
(800) 514-4401
www.bromancellars.com
Open Tasting at Tasting on Main (St Helena), Daily 10:30-6
www.tastingonmain.com

Buehler Vineyards
820 Greenfield Road, St. Helena, CA 94574
(707) 963-2155
buehlers@pacbell.net
www.buehlervineyards.com
Tasting by Appointment, Mon-Fri 10-4

Buena Vista Carneros Winery
18000 Old Winery Road, Sonoma, CA 95476
(800) 926-1266
bvw_info@buenavistawinery.com
www.buenavistawinery.com
Open Tasting, Mon-Fri 10-5, Sat-Sun 10-5:30

Cain Vineyard & Winery
3800 Langtry Road, St. Helena, CA 94574
(707) 963-1616
winery@cainfive.com
www.cainfive.com
Tasting by Appointment, Scheduled Twice Weekly

Ceja Vineyards
1016 Las Amigas Road, Napa, CA 94559
(707) 255-3954 or (877) 633-3954
wine@cejavineyards.com
www.cejavineyards.com
Tasting by Appointment

Chappellet Vineyard & Winery
1581 Sage Canyon Road, St. Helena, CA 94574
(800) 4 - WINERY (494-6379)
toursandtastings@chappellet.com
www.chappellet.com
www.dogsuncorked.com
Tasting by Reservation, Mon-Sat

Chateau Boswell Winery
3468 Silverado Trail, St. Helena, CA 94574
(707) 963-5472
josh@chateauboswellwinery.com
www.chateauboswellwinery.com
Tasting by Appointment

Clark - Claudon Vineyards
wine@clarkclaudon.com
www.clarkclaudon.com

Clos Du Val
5330 Silverado Trail, Napa, CA 94558
(707) 261-5200
cdv@closduval.com
www.closduval.com
Open Tasting, Daily 10-5

CONSTANT–Diamond Mountain Vineyard and Winery
2121 Diamond Mountain Road, Calistoga, CA 94515
(707) 942-0707
info@constantwine.com
www.constantwine.com
Wild Rides and Tasting by Appointment

Corison Winery
987 St. Helena Highway, St. Helena, CA 94574
(707) 963-0826
bob@corison.com
www.corison.com
Tasting by Appointment, Daily 10-5

Crichton Hall Vineyard
1150 Darms Lane, Napa, CA 94558
(707) 224-4200
info@crichtonhall.com
www.crichtonhall.com
Open Tasting at Napa Wine Merchants in Napa, CA, Mon-Sat 10-5

Delectus Winery
908 Enterprise Way #C, Napa, CA 94558
(707) 255-1252
New winery opening 2008:
15300 Ida Clayton Road, Calistoga, CA 95448
admin@delectuswinery.com
www.delectuswinery.com
Tasting by Appointment, Mon-Fri

Domaine Charbay Winery & Distillery
4001 Spring Mtn. Road, St. Helena, CA 94574
(800) 634-7845
info@charbay.com
www.charbay.com
Visits by Appointment, Mon-Sat

Domaine La Due
1623 Bryce Court, Napa, CA 94558
(866) 383-9463
angela@domaineladue.com
www.domaineladue.com
Private Tasting Available

Dutch Henry Winery
4310 Silverado Trail, Calistoga, CA 94515
(888) 224-5879
info@dutchhenry.com
www.dutchhenry.com
Tasting by Appointment, Daily 10-5

Ehlers Estate
3222 Ehlers Lane, St. Helena, CA 94574
(707) 963-5972
info@ehlersestate.com
www.ehlersestate.com
Open Tasting, Daily 10-5

Elkhorn Peak Cellars
200 Polson Road, P.O. Box 821, Napa, CA 94558
(888) 829-5082
www.elkhornpeakcellars.com

Elyse Winery
2100 Hoffman Lane, Napa, CA 94558
(707) 944-2900
info@elysewinery.com
www.elysewinery.com
Tasting by Appointment

Frazier Winery
40 Lupine Hill Road, Napa, CA 94558
(707) 255-3444
sales@frazierwinery.com
www.frazierwinery.com
Tasting by Appointment, Mon-Fri 8:30-6, Sat 9-5

Gargiulo Vineyards
575 Oakville Crossroad, Napa, CA 94558
(707) 944-2770
sharon@gargiulovineyards.com
www.gargiulovineyards.com
Tasting by Appointment

Goosecross Cellars
1119 State Lane, Yountville, CA 94599
(800) 276-9210
hospitality@goosecross.com (Yountville tasting room)
www.goosecross.com
Tasting by Appointment, Daily 10-4:30

Graeser Estate & Winery
255 Petrified Forest Road, Calistoga, CA 94515
(707) 942-4437
richard@graeserwinery.com
www.graeserwinery.com

Grgich Hills Cellar
1829 St. Helena Hwy, Rutherford, CA 94573
(800) 532-3057
info@grgich.com
www.grgich.com
Open Tasting, Daily 9:30-4:30

Groth Vineyards & Winery
750 Oakville Cross Road, Oakville, CA 94562
(707) 944-0290
info@grothwines.com
www.grothwines.com
Tasting by Appointment, Mon-Sat 10-4

Guilliams Vineyards
3851 Spring Mountain Road, St. Helena, CA 94574
(707) 963-9059
www.guilliams.com
Tasting by Appointment

Hess Collection Winery
4411 Redwood Road, Napa, CA 94558
(877) 707-HESS (4377)
info@hesscollection.com
www.hesscollection.com
Open Tasting, Daily 10-4

Honig Vineyard & Winery
850 Rutherford Road, Rutherford, CA 94573
(800) 929-2217
tastings@honigwine.com
www.honigwine.com
Tasting by Appointment, Daily 10-4

Kelham Vineyards
360 Zinfandel Lane, St. Helena, CA 94574
(707) 963-2000
info@kelhamvineyards.com
www.kelhamvineyards.com
Tasting by Appointment

Kirkland Ranch Winery
One Kirkland Ranch Road, Napa, CA 94558
(707) 254-9100
info@kirklandranchwinery.com
www.kirklandranchwinery.com
Tasting by Appointment, 10-4

Kuleto Estate Family Vineyards
2470 Sage Canyon Road, St. Helena, CA 94574
(707) 963-9750
info@kuletoestate.com
www.kuletoestate.com
Tasting by Appointment, Mon-Sat 10:30 & 2:30

Livingston Moffett Winery
1895 Cabernet Lane, St. Helena, CA 94574
(800) 788-0370
info@livingstonwines.com
www.livingstonwines.com
Tasting by Appointment

Madonna Estate Winery
5400 Old Sonoma Road, Napa, CA 94559
(707) 255-8864
mail@madonnaestate.com
www.madonnaestate.com
Open Tasting, Daily 10-5

Miner Family Vineyards
7850 Silverado Trail, Oakville, CA 94562
(800) 366-WINE (9463)
sales@minerwines.com
www.minerwines.com
Open Tasting, Daily 11-5

Monticello Vineyards
4242 Big Ranch Road, Napa, CA 94558
(707) 253-2802
wine@corleyfamilynapavalley.com
www.corleyfamilynapavalley.com
Open Tasting, Daily 10-4:30

Oakville Ranch Vineyards
7781 Silverado Trail, Napa, CA 94558
(707) 944-9665
info@oakvilleranchvineyards.com
www.oakvilleranchvineyards.com
Open Tasting at Tasting on Main (St Helena), Daily 10:30-6

Plumpjack Winery
620 Oakville Cross Road, Oakville, CA 94562
(707) 945-1220
winery@plumpjack.com
www.plumpjack.com
Open Tasting, Daily 10-4

Provenance Vineyards
1695 St. Helena Highway, Rutherford, CA 94573
(707) 968-3633
info@provenancevineyards.com
www.provenancevineyards.com
Open Tasting, Daily 10-4:30

Quintessa
1601 Silverado Trail, Rutherford, CA 94573
(707) 967-1601
info@quintessa.com
www.quintessa.com
Tasting by Appointment, Daily 10-4

Regusci Winery
5584 Silverado Trail, Napa, CA 94558
(707) 254-0403
info@regusciwinery.com
www.regusciwinery.com
Tasting by Appointment, Daily 10-5

Robert Keenan Winery
3660 Spring Mountain Road, St. Helena, CA 94574
(707) 963-9177
rkw@keenanwinery.com
www.keenanwinery.com
Open Tasting, Sat-Sun 11-4
Tasting by Appointment, Mon-Fri

Rombauer Vineyards
3522 Silverado Trail, St. Helena, CA 94574
(800) 622-2206
sheanar@rombauervineyards.com
www.rombauer.com
Open Tasting, Daily 10-5

Rudd Vineyards & Winery
500 Oakville Crossroad, Oakville, CA 94562
(707) 944-8577
info@ruddwines.com
www.ruddwines.com
Tasting by Appointment

RustRidge Ranch & Winery
2910 Lower Chiles Valley Road, St. Helena, CA 94574
(707) 965-9353
RustRidge@RustRidge.com
www.RustRidge.com
Open Tasting, Daily 10-4

Saddleback Cellars
7802 Money Road, Oakville, CA 94562
(707) 944-1305
hillery@saddlebackcellars.com
www.saddlebackcellars.com
Tasting by Appointment, Mon-Sat

Saintsbury
1500 Los Carneros Avenue, Napa, CA 94559
(707) 252-0592
info@saintsbury.com
www.saintsbury.com
Tasting by Appointment, Mon-Fri

Salvestrin Estate Vineyard and Winery
397 Main Street, St. Helena, CA 94574
(707) 963-5105
shannon@salvestrinwinery.com
www.salvestrinwinery.com
Tasting by Appointment

Schweiger Vineyards
4015 Spring Mtn. Road, St. Helena, CA 94574
(877) 963-4882
svwine@schweigervineyards.com
www.schweigervineyards.com
Tasting by Appointment

S.E. Chase Family Cellars
PO Box 508, St. Helena, CA 94574
(707) 963-1284
mail@chasecellars.com
www.chasecellars.com
Tasting by Appointment

Sequoia Grove Vineyards and Winery
8338 St. Helena Highway, Rutherford, CA 94558
(800) 851-7841
info@sequoiagrove.com
www.sequoiagrove.com
Open Tasting, Daily 10:30-5

Shafer Vineyards
6154 Silverado Trail, Napa, CA 94558
(707) 944-2877
info@shafervineyards.com
www.shafervineyards.com
Tasting by Appointment, Mon-Fri 10-2

Signorello Vineyards
4500 Silverado Trail, Napa, CA 94558
(707) 255-5990
info@signorellovineyards.com
www.signorellovineyards.com
Open Tasting, Daily 10:30-5

Spottswoode Estate Vineyard & Winery
1902 Madrona Avenue, St. Helena, CA 94574
(707) 963-0134
spottswoode@spottswoode.com
www.spottswoode.com
Tasting by Appointment, Tue & Fri at 10:00

Staglin Family Vineyard
PO Box 680, Rutherford, CA 94573
(707) 944-0477
info@staglinfamily.com
www.staglinfamily.com
Tasting by Appointment

Steltzner Vineyards
5998 Silverado Trail, Napa, CA 94558
(707) 252-7272
wines@steltzner.com
www.steltzner.com
Tasting by Appointment, Daily

Stony Hill Vineyard
PO Box 308, St. Helena, CA 94574
(707) 963-2636
www.stonyhillvineyard.com
Tasting by Appointment, Mon-Fri 9-5

Sullivan Vineyards
1090 Galleron Road, Rutherford, CA 94573
(877) 244-7337
www.sullivanwine.com
Tasting by Appointment, Daily 10-5

TOR Wines
Kenward Family Vineyards
1241 Adams Street, Suite 1045, St. Helena, CA 94574
(707) 963-3100
info@torwines.com
www.torwines.com
Private Tasting Available

Trahan Winery
www.trahanwinery.com
chuck@trahanwinery.com
(707) 342-1364
Tasting by Appointment

V. Sattui Winery
1111 White Lane, St. Helena, CA 94574
(707) 963-7774
info@vsattui.com
www.vsattui.com
Open Tasting, Daily 9-5 (Winter), 9-6 (Summer)

Van Der Heyden Vineyards
4057 Silverado Trail, Napa, CA 94558
(707) 257-0130
talig@vanderheydenvineyards.com
www.vanderheydenvineyards.com
Tasting by Appointment, Daily 10-6

Venge Vineyards
424 Crystal Springs Road, St. Helena, CA 94573
(707) 967-1008
info@vengevineyards.com
www.vengevineyards.com
Tasting by Appointment, Daily 10-5

Varozza Vineyards
514 Pratt Avenue, St. Helena, CA 94574
(707) 963-0331
www.varozzavineyards.com
Tasting by Appointment

Vincent Arroyo Winery
2361 Greenwood Ave., Calistoga, CA 94515
(707) 942-6995
www.vincentarroyo.com
Open Tasting, Daily 10-4:30

Whitehall Lane Winery
1563 St. Helena Hwy, St. Helena, CA 94574
(800) 963-9454
greatwine@whitehalllane.com
www.whitehalllane.com
Open Tasting, Daily 11-5:45

William Hill Winery
1761 Atlas Peak Road, Napa, CA 94558
(707) 224-5424
whw_info@williamhillwinery.com
www.williamhill.com
Tasting by Appointment, Daily 10:30-4

Zahtila Vineyards
2250 Lake County Highway, Calistoga, CA 94515
(707) 942-9251
sales@zahtilavineyards.com
www.zahtilavineyards.com
Tasting by Appointment

Photography assistant-in-training
Zack Zundel

Kitty Crossing
Regusci Winery

Scenic Kuleto Estate Family Vineyards

Freddy Constant with Caso & Floozy
CONSTANT–Diamond Mountain Vineyard
and Winery

Amelia Ceja
Ceja Vineyards

Riley fetching the paper
Acacia Vineyard

Winery Dogs cofounder, Allen Jacoby, hard
at work

Dick Steltzner with Finder & Magnus
Steltzner Vineyards

Plado tasting from the filter press
S.E. Chase Family Cellars

Distillery
Domaine Charbay Winery & Distillery

Sadie and Gary Koehler singing
Dutch Henry Winery

Steve Allen with Dizzy driving the forklift
Sequoia Grove Vineyards and Winery

A non-canine friend
RustRidge Ranch & Winery

The Bartolucci Family
Madonna Estate Winery

Frank Altamura & Woody
Altamura Winery & Vineyards

Earl going for a ride
Bouchaine Vineyards

Winemaker Rudy Zuidema getting a kiss from Ripley
Ehlers Estate

Photography assistant Jake Zundel

One of the sweetest dogs we met, Maidchen, of Goosecross Cellars, passed away beneath her favorite vine before the book was published. She lived to a very old age for a Great Dane and enjoyed an ideal life at the vineyard. We are grateful for the chance to have met such a beautiful soul.